do some readings —
clarinet, go down the
players — go talk to
Bassoon + share
them.
Horn   same both

Enigma Variations
and
Pomp and Circumstance Marches

Enigma Variations
and
Pomp and Circumstance Marches
in Full Score

EDWARD ELGAR

Dover Publications, Inc.
New York

Published in Canada by General Publishing Company, Ltd., 30 Lesmill Road, Don Mills, Toronto, Ontario.

This Dover edition, first published in 1992, is an unabridged republication of *Variations on an Original Theme ("Enigma")*, first published by Novello & Co., London, in 1899, and *Pomp and Circumstance Marches* 1–4, first published by Boosey & Co., London, in 1902 (Nos. 1 and 2), 1905 and 1907.

Manufactured in the United States of America
Dover Publications, Inc., 31 East 2nd Street, Mineola, N.Y. 11501

Library of Congress Cataloging-in-Publication Data

Elgar, Edward, 1857–1934.
    [Variations on an original theme]
    Enigma variations ; and, Pomp and circumstance marches / Edward Elgar. — In full score.
    1 score.
    For orchestra.
    Reprint (1st work). Originally published: London : Novello, 1899.
    Reprint (2nd work). Originally published: London : Boosey, 1902–1907.
    ISBN 0-486-27342-3
    1. Variations (Orchestra)—Scores. 2. Marches (Orchestra)—Scores.
I. Elgar, Edward, 1857–1934. Pomp and circumstance. 1992. II. Title:
Enigma variations. III. Title: Pomp and circumstance marches.
M1000.E43V4 1992   92-758508
                                                          CIP

M

_organ-
bass - frees the
cellos_

CONTENTS

   *The identifications of the friends depicted in the variations are as follows, by number:
   I: Caroline Alice Elgar, his wife. II: Hew David Steuart-Powell, amateur pianist. III: Richard Baxter Townshend, author. IV: W. M. Baker, "country squire, gentleman and scholar." V: Richard P. Arnold, son of Matthew Arnold, amateur pianist. VI: Isabel (not "Ysobel") Fitton, amateur violist. VII: Troyte Griffith, architect, piano student of Elgar. VIII: Winifred Norbury, amateur musician. IX: A. J. Jaeger, office manager at Novello. X: Dora Penny. XI: George Robertson Sinclair, organist of Hereford Cathedral. XII: Basil G. Nevinson, amateur cellist. XIII: Lady Mary Lygon. XIV: Elgar himself (the initials are "a paraphrase of a fond name").

INSTRUMENTATION

ENIGMA VARIATIONS

2 Flutes [Flauti; Fl.]
  (Fl. II = Piccolo [Picc.])
2 Oboes [Oboi; Ob.]
2 Clarinets (Bb) [Clarinetti in Bb; Cl.]
2 Bassoons [Fagotti; Fg.]
Contrabassoon [Contra Fagotto; C. Fg.]
4 Horns (F) [Corni in F; Cor.]
3 Trumpets (F) [Trombe in F; Tr.]
3 Trombones [Tromboni; Tromb.]
Tuba [Tuba]
Timpani [Timpani; Timp.]
Side Drum [Tamburo piccolo; Tamb. picc.]
Triangle [Triangolo; Triang.]
Bass Drum [Gran Cassa; G. C.]
Cymbals [Piatti]
Organ [Organo] *ad lib.*
Violins I, II [Violini; Viol.]
Violas [Viole]
Cellos [Violoncelli; Vcl.]
Basses [Bassi]

POMP AND CIRCUMSTANCE MARCHES

NO. 1

1 or 2 Piccolos [Piccolo]
2 Flutes [Flauti]
2 Oboes [Oboi]
2 Clarinets (A) [Clarinetti in A]
Bass Clarinet (A) [Clarinetto Basso in A]
2 Bassoons [Fagotti]
Contrabassoon [Contra-Fagotto]
4 Horns (F) [Corni in F]
2 Trumpets (F) [Trombe in F]
2 Cornets (A) [Cornetti in A]
3 Trombones [Tromboni]
Tuba [Tuba]
Timpani [Timpani]
Bass Drum [Gran Cassa; G. C.]
Piatti [Cymbals]
Triangle [Triangolo; Trgl.]

Side Drum [Tamburo piccolo]
Jingles [Schellen]
Tambourine
Glockenspiel [Glockensp.] *ad lib.*
2 Harps [Arpa]
Organ [Organo]
Violins I, II [Violini]
Violas [Viole]
Cellos [Violoncelli]
Basses [Bassi]

NO. 2

Piccolo [Piccolo]
2 Flutes [Flauti]
2 Oboes [Oboi]
2 Clarinets (A) [Clarinetti in A]
Bass Clarinet (A) [Clarinetto basso in A]
2 Bassoons [Fagotti]
Contrabassoon [Contra-Fagotto]
4 Horns (F) [Corni in F]
2 Trumpets (F) [Trombe in F]
2 Cornets (A) [Cornetti in A]
3 Trombones [Tromboni]
Tuba [Tuba]
Timpani [Timpani]
1 or 2 Side Drums [Tamburo piccolo; Tamb.]
Triangle [Triangolo; Triang.]
Glockenspiel [Glock.] } Bells [Campanelli]
Jingles [Schellen]
Bass Drum [Gran Cassa; G. C.]
Cymbals [Piatti]
Violins I, II [Violini]
Violas [Viole]
Cellos [Violoncelli]
Basses [Bassi]

NO. 3

Piccolo [Piccolo]
2 Flutes [Flauti]
2 Oboes [Oboi]
English Horn [Corno Inglese]
2 Clarinets (Bb) [Clarinetti in Bb]
Bass Clarinet (Bb) [Clarinetto Basso in Bb]

3 Bassoons [Fagotti]
Contrabassoon [Contra-Fagotto]
4 Horns (F) [Corni in F]
2 Trumpets (B♭) [Trombe in B♭]
2 Cornets (B♭) [Cornetti in B♭]
3 Trombones [Tromboni]
Tuba [Tuba]
Timpani [Timpani]
Tenor Drum [Tamburo tenore]
Side Drum [Tamburo piccolo]
Bass Drum [Gran Cassa]
Cymbals [Piatti]
Violins I, II [Violini]
Violas [Viole]
Cellos [Violoncelli]
Basses [Bassi]

NO. 4

3 Flutes [Flauti]
   (Fl. III = Piccolo [Piccolo])

2 Oboes [Oboi]
English Horn [Cor. Inglese]
2 Clarinets (B♭) [Clarinetti in B]
Bass Clarinet (B♭) [Clarinetto basso in B]
2 Bassoons [Fagotti]
Contrabassoon [Contra-Fagotto]
4 Horns (F) [Corni in F]
3 Trumpets (A) [Trombe in A]
3 Trombones [Tromboni]
Tuba [Tuba]
Timpani [Timpani]
Side Drum [Tamburo piccolo]
Bass Drum [Gran Cassa]
Cymbals [Piatti]
2 Harps [Arpe]
Violins I, II [Violini]
Violas [Viole]
Cellos [Violoncelli]
Basses [Bassi]

Enigma Variations
and
Pomp and Circumstance Marches

ENIGMA VARIATIONS
(Variations on an Original Theme)
Op. 36

II.
(H.D.S-P.)

IV.
(W. M. B.)

VI.
(Ysobel.)

X.
(Dorabella.)
Intermezzo.

40

41

*) Dieser Takt wird nur im Falle einer Separat
Aufführung dieser Var. XII gespielt.

*) This bar should be omitted except
when Var. XII is played separately.

XIII.
(* * *)
Romanza.

POMP AND CIRCUMSTANCE MARCH NO. 1

Op. 39, No. 1

*) NB. The words in parentheses are for the guidance of the Conductor only; they are not printed in the orchestral parts.

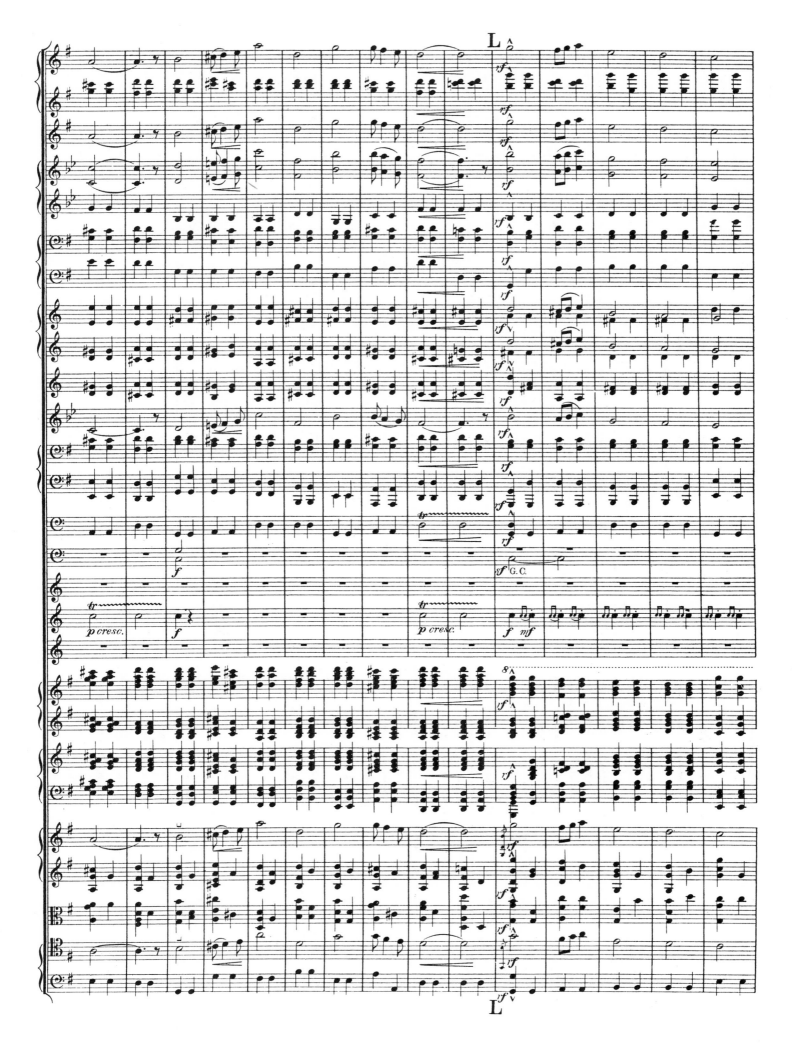

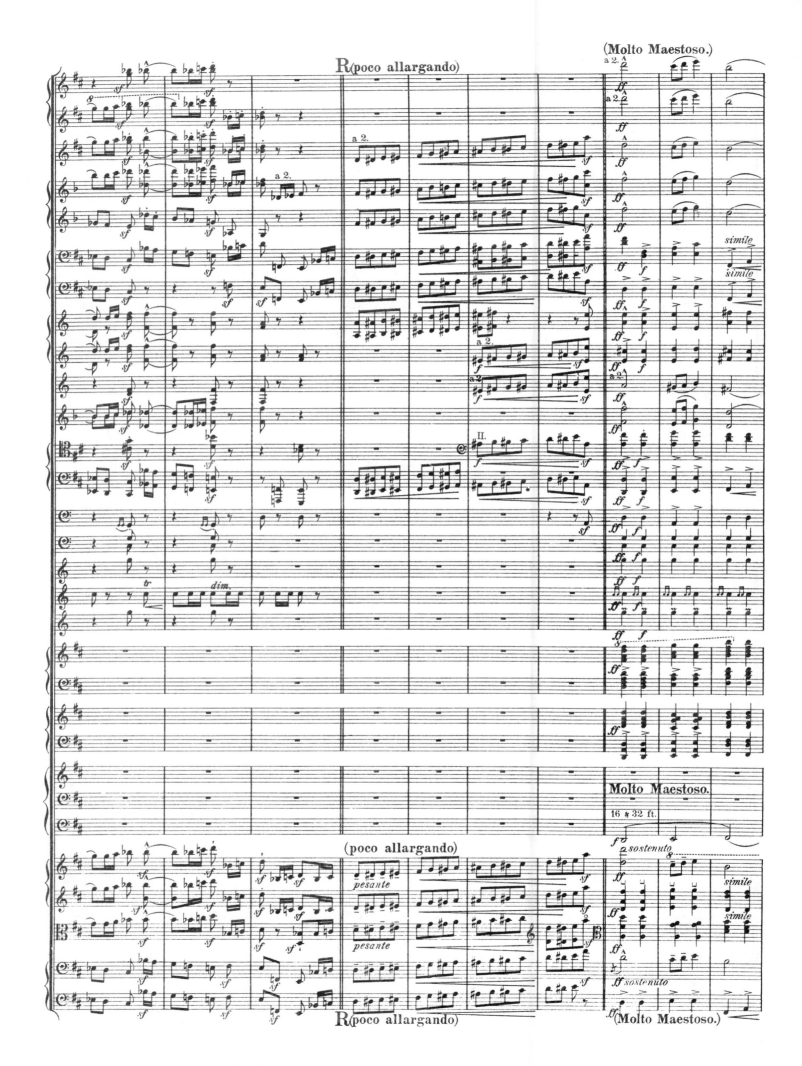

(allargando)

(allargando)

POMP AND CIRCUMSTANCE MARCH NO. 2

Op. 39, No. 2

*) La seconda volta (*D. C.*) senza repetizione.

CODA.

POMP AND CIRCUMSTANCE MARCH NO. 3
Op. 39, No. 3

*) The tone of the Fagotti must be allowed to preponderate in this and corresponding passages.

poco allarg.

poco allargando

poco allargando

poco allargando

188　Pomp and Circumstance March No. 3

POMP AND CIRCUMSTANCE MARCH NO. 4

Op. 39, No. 4